DK READERS

Pre-Level 1

Big Trucks
Colorful Days
Farm Animals
Fishy Tales
Garden Friends
In the Park
Meet the Dinosaurs
Monkeys
My Day
Petting Zoo
Ponies and Horses
Snakes Slither and Hiss
John Deere: Busy Tractors

LEGO® DUPLO: On the Farm
Star Wars The Clone Wars: Don't Wake the
  Zillo Beast!
Star Wars The Clone Wars: Masters of the
  Force
Star Wars: Blast Off!
Star Wars: Even Droids Need Friends

Level 1

Animal Hide and Seek
Animals at Home
A Bed for the Winter
Big Machines
Born to be a Butterfly
Bugs and Us
Busy Buzzy Bee
A Day at Greenhill Farm
A Day in the Life of a Builder
A Day in the Life of a Firefighter
A Day in the Life of a Police Officer
A Day in the Life of a Teacher
Dinosaur's Day
Diving Dolphin
Duckling Days
Feeding Time
First Day at Gymnastics
Homes Around the World
I Want to Be a Ballerina
Let's Play Soccer
Rockets and Spaceships
Submarines and Submersibles
Surprise Puppy!
Tale of a Tadpole
Train Travel
A Trip to the Dentist
A Trip to the Zoo
Truck Trouble
Whatever the Weather
Wild Baby Animals
Angry Birds Star Wars: Yoda Bird's Heroes
Indiana Jones: Indy's Adventures
John Deere: Good Morning, Farm!
LEGO® DC Super Heroes: Ready for
  Action!

LEGO® DUPLO: Around Town
LEGO® Pirates: Brickbeard's Treasure
Star Wars The Clone Wars: Ahsoka in
  Action
Star Wars The Clone Wars: Pirates . . . and
  Worse!
Star Wars The Clone Wars: Watch Out for
  Jabba the Hutt!
Star Wars: Luke Skywalker's Amazing Story
Star Wars: Ready, Set, Podrace!
Star Wars: Tatooine Adventures
Star Wars: What is a Wookiee?
Star Wars: Who Saved the Galaxy?

A Note to Parents

DK READERS is a compelling program for beginning readers, designed in conjunction with leading literacy experts, including Dr. Linda Gambrell, Distinguished Professor of Education at Clemson University. Dr. Gambrell has served as President of the National Reading Conference, the College Reading Association, and the International Reading Association.

Beautiful illustrations and superb full-color photographs combine with engaging, easy-to-read stories to offer a fresh approach to each subject in the series. Each DK READER is guaranteed to capture a child's interest while developing his or her reading skills, general knowledge, and love of reading.

The five levels of DK READERS are aimed at different reading abilities, enabling you to choose the books that are exactly right for your child:

Pre-level 1: Learning to read
Level 1: Beginning to read
Level 2: Beginning to read alone
Level 3: Reading alone
Level 4: Proficient readers

The "normal" age at which a child begins to read can be anywhere from three to eight years old. Adult participation through the lower levels is very helpful for providing encouragement, discussing storylines, and sounding out unfamiliar words.

No matter which level you select, you can be sure that you are helping your child learn to read, then read to learn!

LONDON, NEW YORK, MUNICH,
MELBOURNE, and DELHI

Editor Lisa Stock
Designer Carol Davis
Art Editor Toby Truphet
Managing Editor Laura Gilbert
Design Manager Maxine Pedliham
Publishing Manager Julie Ferris
Publishing Director Simon Beecroft
Pre-Production Producer Marc Staples
Reading Consultant Dr. Linda Gambrell

For Lucasfilm
Executive Editor J.W. Rinzler
Art Director Troy Alders
Keeper of the Holocron Leland Chee
Director of Publishing Carol Roeder

First American Edition, 2013
13 14 15 16 10 9 8 7 6 5 4 3 2 1
001-187885-Nov/13

Published in the United States by
DK Publishing
345 Hudson Street, New York, New York 10014

Published in Great Britain by Dorling Kindersley Limited

A catalog record for this book is available
from the Library of Congress.

ISBN: 978-1-4654-0182-3 (Paperback)
ISBN: 978-1-4654-0183-0 (Hardcover)

Color reproduction by Altaimage, UK
Printed and bound by L-Rex Printing Co., Ltd, China

Discover more at
www.dk.com

Contents

DK READERS

LEARNING
pre-level
1
TO READ

STAR WARS

EVEN DROIDS
NEED FRIENDS

Written by Simon Beecroft

The *Star Wars* galaxy
is a place where great
adventures happen.

Along the way, great
friendships are made
as well.

Some friends
make a
great team.

Anakin
Skywalker
is fearless.

Obi-Wan
Kenobi
is very wise.

Together
they are
unbeatable.

Some friends love doing the same things.

Han Solo and Chewbacca both love flying spaceships.

Spaceships

Some friends don't like each other at first.

Luke thinks Han is a
show-off.

Han thinks Luke is
just a kid.

But soon they become
best friends.

Some friends have the same enemies.

Stormtroopers

Princess Leia and
Wicket both want
to defeat the
stormtroopers.

argue a lot.

Best friends R2-D2
and C-3PO argue
almost all of
the time!

Some friends have
known each other for
a long time.

Anakin is nine years old
when he meets Padmé.

She is fourteen.

Some friends have their ups and downs.

Lando Calrissian tricks Han, but they become friends again.

Some friends are double trouble.

Dr. Evazan and Ponda Baba are the worst bullies you ever saw!

Some friends don't know that they want to be friends.

Princess Leia and Han Solo pretend they don't like each other.

But really they love each other!

Some friends look
different than
each other.

Yoda is small
and green.

Chewbacca
is tall and
hairy.

Some friends look alike.

Logray and Chief Chirpa are both Ewoks.

Ewoks

Some friends never let each other down.

These two Jedi look
after each other
in battle.

Who would you most like to be friends with?

Who are you less likely to be friends with?

Glossary

Ewok
A small, furry creature that lives in the forest on the planet of Endor.

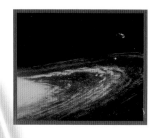

Galaxy
A group of millions of stars and planets.

Jedi
A member of a group with special powers that fights evil.

Stormtrooper
A soldier of an evil army who wears white armor.

Index

DK READERS

My name is

_____

I have read this book

Date

_____